A Craftsman's Handbook

HENRY LAPP

INTRODUCTION & NOTES
BY *Beatrice B. Garvan*
CURATOR EMERITUS *of* AMERICAN ART

W0009502

Good Books®

in cooperation with the
PHILADELPHIA MUSEUM *of* ART

Above: Two versions of Henry Lapp's billhead stamp. No such marks appear on any of the furniture known to have been made by him.

Original design by John Anderson

Design of this edition and slipcase by Dawn J. Ranck

A CRAFTSMAN'S HANDBOOK: HENRY LAPP
Copyright © 1975 by the Philadelphia Museum of Art
International Standard Book Number: 1-56148-014-2
Library of Congress Catalog Card Number: 75-5212
Library of Congress Cataloging-in-Publication Data

Introduction

OF THE HUNDREDS OF CARPENTER-CABINETMAKERS "building" nineteenth century America, none have left such a colorful and precise description of their production as Henry Lapp when he drew and painted examples of his craftsmanship on the pages of his little "handbook." Small, soft, and portable, it fit easily into the pocket; and Henry Lapp must have carried it with him to exhibit samples of his cabinetmaking enterprise to prospective purchasers. Perhaps the unpretentious shape of the store-bought notebook, its plain cover, coarse paper, and simply sewn binding did not attract much attention, for the little handbook lay unnoticed in the drawer of a small bureau which was purchased by a dealer from a descendant of Henry Lapp about 1956. When it was discovered, it was soon sold to an appreciative collector; and it came to the Philadelphia Museum of Art as a gift from Mr. Titus Geesey in 1958. This reproduction of Henry Lapp's handbook follows the original faithfully, with the addition of textual notes which accompany Lapp's drawings.

Henry's father, Michael K. Lapp (October 24, 1830—August 19, 1884), had married Rebecca Lantz in the Amish faith in February 1858. One of several children, Henry L. Lapp was born on August 18, 1862, on a farm at Groff's Store (now Mascot) in Leacock Township, Lancaster County, Pennsylvania. Earlier Amish records show that by 1820 large Lapp families had moved into Leacock and the surrounding communities of Earl, Salisbury, Paradise, and East Lampeter in Lancaster County. Most were listed as farmers; and the rich soil of the area, which produced grain and tobacco of the highest quality, supported communities based on agricultural pursuits. This was Henry Lapp's market. He became a carpenter, working in the Groff's Store area, and was so listed in the Lancaster Directory of 1890.

Born deaf and partially mute, Henry Lapp was in all other respects a bright and enterprising young man, for by 1898 he had moved to his own place on the old "Philly Pike" at Bird-in-Hand and was listed as a cabinetmaker. Here he carried on a carpentry and cabinetmaking business as well as a paint and hardware dealership. The Lancaster County Atlas of 1899 indicates three wooden buildings in his name on the north side of the Philadelphia road, approximately halfway between the villages of Bird-in-Hand and Intercourse. One of these is the L-shaped house where he lived with his sister. Another, a half-stone barn, small by Lancaster standards, sits behind the house. On one of the inside beams, Henry Lapp has scratched his name. Lapp's shop was just east of the other two buildings, and here he sold his products and carried on his work. His saws and lathes were powered by a large windmill which worked efficiently when the wind reached a velocity of five miles or more per hour.

Henry Lapp's furniture designs reflect his life, his skills, and his community. Traditional utilitarian forms, used daily for generations in country households and on farms, as well as games and toys, seed boxes, flower stands, counter boxes, buggies, sleighs, and wagons, give glimpses into the industry, humor, enterprise, and mobility of the people in the heart of the Pennsylvania German farmlands where Lapp was born. At the same time, to supply his trade and store, Lapp made frequent trips to Philadelphia by horse-drawn wagon, following the "Philly Pike" to the Lancaster Turnpike, then east for some sixty miles, over the Schuylkill via the Middle Ferry Bridge, and on to Market Street. Lapp's designs, especially those in this little handbook, clearly illustrate the influence of both aspects of his life. His chests, boxes, and sinks, although typical Lancaster County pieces, were not decorated in the old, Germanic tradition of unicorns and tulips, but rather in broad flat areas of color characteristic of the furniture of the Welsh country settlers who located in Pennsylvania east of Lancaster County, and which Lapp probably saw in country stores and shops near Philadelphia. Perhaps these colors also illustrated what Lapp had to offer in his paint store, which carried the slogan: There is none that equals.

Lapp's desks and washstands are forms not generally found in Pennsylvania German houses, but are typical of urban styles designed for larger houses with rooms reserved for special purposes. His adaptations of the carrot-shaped foot and the bulbous, rounded foot are but variations of design-book models made in rosewood and mahogany by Philadelphia cabinetmakers.

Lapp's neatly penciled drawings and vivid watercolors were perhaps occasioned by his inability to otherwise communicate with customers. His handbook is therefore a personal statement as well as a commercial catalogue; and it has provided us with a unique record of his craftsmanship, his abilities, and his oeuvre. Henry Lapp died on July 5, 1904, from lead poisoning and was buried at Gordonville. Since he died unmarried, his business possessions were sold at auction from his shop shortly after his death. Although unmarked, there are a few extant pieces known to be by him; and the quality of his cabinetmaking is still celebrated in his community.

PLATE I

BLANKET OR DOWER CHEST

Made in all sizes, this traditional and important Pennsylvania German furniture form provided excellent storage for household linens or for a bride's trousseau. The top raises on concealed hinges and fastens with a spring lock. The upper section is separated from the lower drawer by a partition, as indicated by the horizontal molding on the front and sides. Only the compound turned feet date this otherwise timeless piece in the nineteenth century.

DROP LEAF TABLE

Probably intended to be made in large sizes, this dining table has rounded turned legs decorated with incised lines and ending in carrot feet. Versatile and sturdy, it could be used both indoors and out. Although no specific dimensions are given by Lapp throughout the handbook—except for his occasional terms "small" or "little"—one assumes that almost all pieces could be made in different sizes.

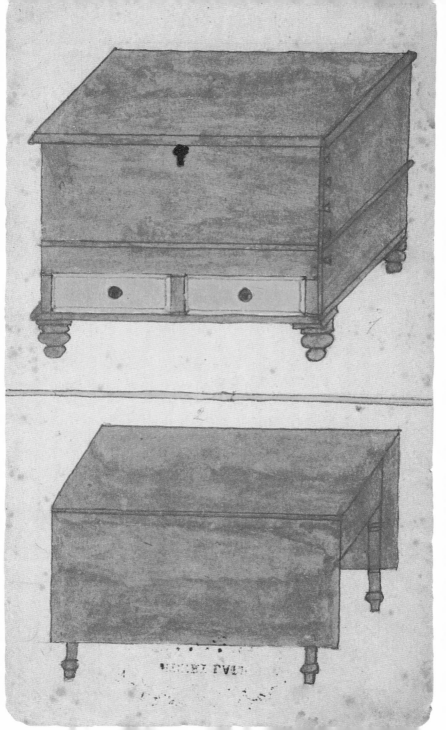

PLATE 2

WALL CUPBOARD
Sometimes called a "dresser," this decorative cupboard held china, cutlery, and linens and was the largest piece of household cabinetry made by Henry Lapp. Pegged mortise and tenon joints on the paneled doors, raised molded panels on drawer fronts, and top and bottom finish molds are indicative of Lapp's correct and traditional cabinetmaking techniques.

PLATE 3

BUREAU

This bureau, with its finely detailed cabinetwork, is very much like the one in which Lapp's little handbook was found. It has raised molded-edged drawers, sunken side panels, and is decoratively painted in two colors, with an indication of free brushwork or sponge painting on the drawer fronts. The handwriting on all illustrations has been identified as Henry Lapp's; numbers may refer to model numbers, probably keyed to a size and price book.

✿

WASHBENCH

An important piece of furniture usually located near the family entry, the washbench was used by "all hands." It was serviced at first by water stored in buckets and pitchers; later, by pumps and faucets. Vegetables, flowers, and flowerpots were scrubbed or soaked in bowls and pans stored in the cupboard below or prepared with utensils tucked into the four side drawers. The two top levels allowed drying space.

No 4

bureau

Washbench 5

PLATE 4

WASHBENCH

Many variations of the washbench form attest to its popularity and probably to its necessity. Those used often for food or dishwashing purposes had top units lined with copper or tin and painted green, as seen in the pieces illustrated here.

❈

WASHBENCH

Slightly varied from the above washbench, this piece had additional drawers, probably for utensils used in fruit and vegetable preparation, either for canning or immediate consumption. Both pieces are straightforward carpentry without the suggestion of dovetails or mortise and tenon joinery, nor do the bases have locked doors.

No 6

Washbench

7

Washbench

PLATE 5

WASHBENCH

This was the simplest form of the washbench and was used on porches and in outbuildings where fruits and vegetables or potted plants received their preliminary preparation. Large sieves, bowls, and baskets could be stored in the swivel-latched cupboards below.

❊

WASHBENCH

Painted oval panels on the doors and drawers in graduated sizes give this washbench added design distinction, even though simple carpentry is still indicated. The hinged lid provided a working surface as well as a cover for the compartment beneath, keeping its contents dry and clean.

PLATE 6

DESK

The three drawers in this desk may indicate a diminutive size, for the other desks and chests drawn by Lapp have four or five drawers more typical of the form. The brass escutcheon and its cover stand out brightly against the basic barn red with blue-red decorated lid and drawer fronts. One of Lapp's more ambitious designs, this desk reflects his urban contacts.

TABLE

Unequal drawers and a wide overhanging top are typical of the Pennsylvania table, whether made in the city or the country. This example has the same turned incised legs as those on the drop leaf table, Plate 1, but here the carrot-shaped feet terminate in casters, a useful if curious addition—probably the result of Lapp's hardware trade.

desk. 24

10

table

PLATE 7

CUPBOARD

A multipurpose unit, this cupboard could be used in bedrooms to hold pitchers, washbowls, and commodes, or clothes neatly folded in interior shelves. In a country parlor or kitchen, it might store linens. The simple closing latch was maneuverable by all ages.

❁

WOOD CHEST

Made in all sizes to store smaller pieces of dry firewood and stovewood, Lapp's use of large dovetailing at the corners makes an attractive and strong joint for a box destined for hard use. The hinged, lidded top kept moisture out and served as a bench.

26

cupboard

17

wood chest

PLATE 8

DRAWER

Thoroughly recognizable as Lapp's work in the details of its paneled and painted drawer fronts, flush cove–molded top, and compound turned feet, this piece is usually called a chest of drawers.

✷

BENCH

This bench form, which makes a feature of the open mortise and tenon joint between the top and the legs, was a carpentry item made all over Pennsylvania especially for use on porches and in meetinghouses.

✷

BENCH

Two examples of the simplest form of the bench—the round one was probably small; the other could be any length where a single plank was useful. Wedges hold the legs firmly in bored holes.

12

drawer

bench

bench

PLATE 9

DESK

This piece is very similar in all construction details to the desk in Plate 6, but the addition of a fourth drawer and a base molding along the sides, front to back, suggests a more expensive desk. The feet are clearly drawn and are typical nineteenth century versions of the turnip shape found on many earlier Pennsylvania German pieces.

SALTBOX

An important household commodity, salt was purchased in solid units, pounded to its granular form, and "pinched" by the cook from hanging units such as these saltboxes. Of simple construction, the saltbox on the left has a drawer section which probably held a scoop or small chopper to loosen the salt.

desk 25

desk.

salt.box.

PLATE 10

BEDSTEAD

Although the perspective is far from precise in Lapp's drawing for this bedstead, all the decorative details of incised lines, terminal post knobs, carved headboard, and turned rope pegs are clear. This was the most elaborate bed Lapp designed.

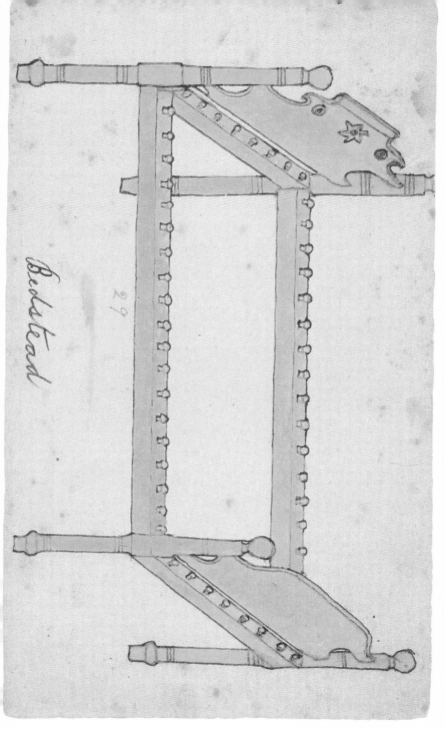

Bedstead

29

PLATE 11

BEDSTEAD

This simple version of the bedstead, which could be made in single, three-quarter, and double sizes, was probably for a child. Constructed exactly like the previous example, it lacks only the elaborations on the headboard and legs.

❂

CRADLE

A very simple cradle like this might be used in warm rooms where drafts were controlled. Its open top allowed Baby to be amused when awake by household activities he could see going on around him.

❂

LITTLE CRADLE; LITTLE BEDSTEAD

Diminutive sizes of cradles and bedsteads for her dolls to please a budding housekeeper.

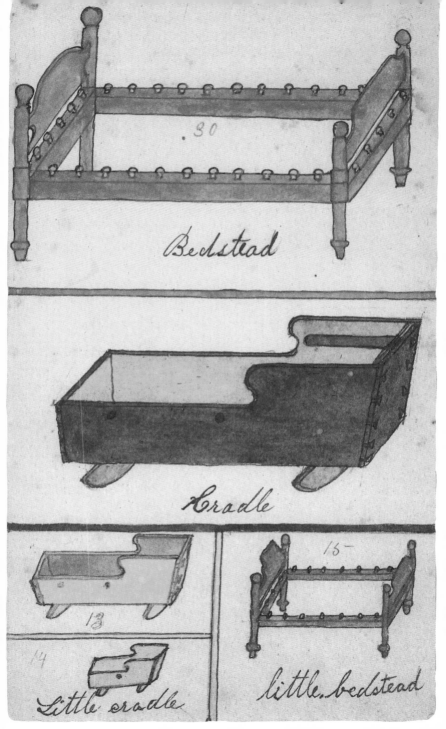

Bedstead

Cradle

Little cradle

little bedstead

PLATE 12

DOUGH TABLE

Dough tables were made in all sizes, as permanent table-like pieces or for portable use without legs. They were sturdily constructed with dovetailed joints and side pieces set into the bottom board to make them moisture tight. Large quantities of dough were kneaded and molded on the top, set back into the table, covered, and left to rise. The legs were always splayed and sometimes braced with stretchers for stability.

FLOUR CHEST

The flour chest was built like a large bin, about 30 inches high, 40 inches wide, and 24 inches deep. Flour was dumped in from sacks carted from the grinding mills. From this chest it was scooped out, sifted, and worked, perhaps on the dough table.

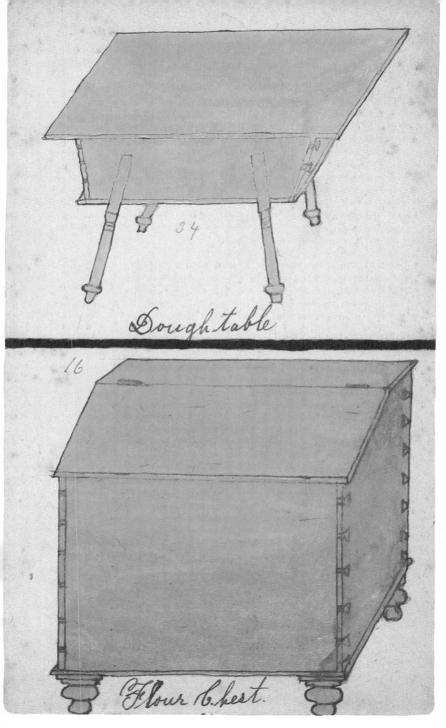

34

Dough table

16

Flour Chest.

PLATE 13

FLOUR CHEST

This flour chest has the addition of a neat cupboard in the bottom in which the dough tray and other sieves and scoops could be stored. Simple swivel wood closures kept the doors shut. The dough tray, below, was designed to fit into the flour chest. It was constructed exactly like its larger counterpart in Plate 12, but lacks legs. The cutout endpieces make handles for easy carrying, and the bread could be worked wherever temperature or comfort determined—by the hearth in winter or under a shady tree in summer.

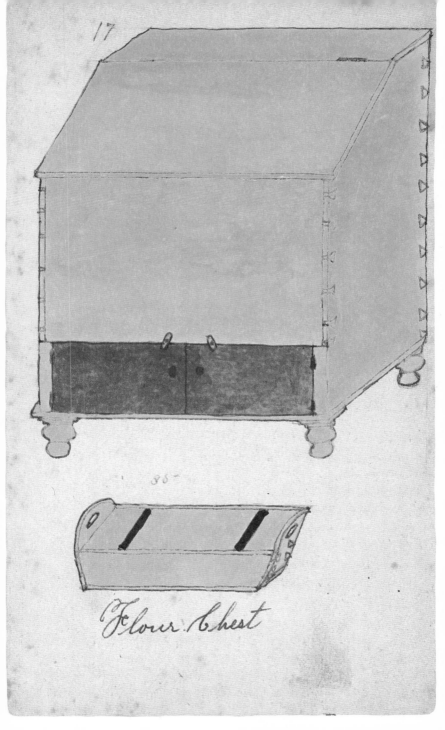

17

Flour Chest

PLATE 14

FLOUR CHEST

Slightly varied from the preceding example, this flour chest has a flat top which could serve as a table for the dough tray stored underneath. Bread baking was usually a weekly task and required utensils and containers which could handle large quantities of ingredients.

DESK

This desk has the same construction details as the slope front flour chests. The interior section under the lid was a storage well for papers, bills, and receipts. Writing was accomplished with the lid in a closed position; thus it was possible to make entries in ledgers or write receipts without having all one's business "open." This desk shows the cabinetmaker's care, with pinned mortise and tenon joints and a brass escutcheon. Square tapered legs indicate Lapp's nineteenth century heritage as does his use of turned members on other designs.

18

Flour Chest.

36

Desk

PLATE 15

DESK

The design of this desk is unusual in that the lid drops down on supports which pull out, but the inside compartment is still well-like (see Plate 23). Movable parts are painted in the blue-red pattern while framework remains plain barn red.

❂

READING TABLE

A simple podium, or lectern, this slope front table has no interior compartments. The legs are typical Lapp creations, turned and ringed with carrot feet. These tables were used in meetinghouses and public halls, sometimes in schoolrooms, and, if high enough, as writing tables for the large ledgers kept in mills and stores.

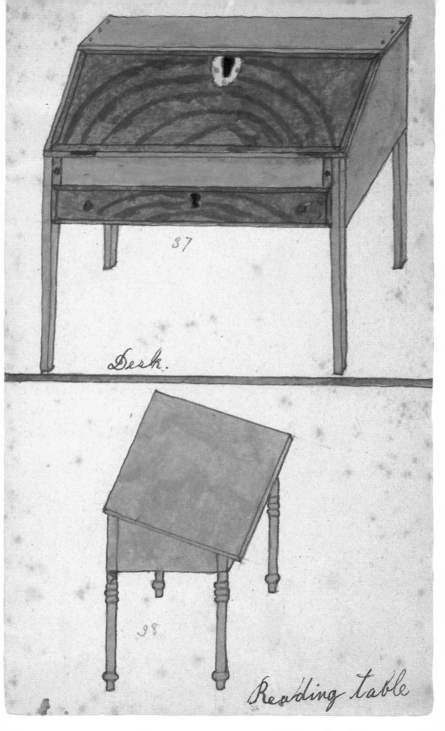

37

Desk.

38

Reading table

PLATE 16

SETTEE

A simple, sturdy, and well-designed country settee was the most commodious seating facility on porches and parlors, in churches and schools. Always painted, sometimes stenciled or "marbled," it withstood weather and weight, remaining one of the most versatile pieces produced by the American craftsman.

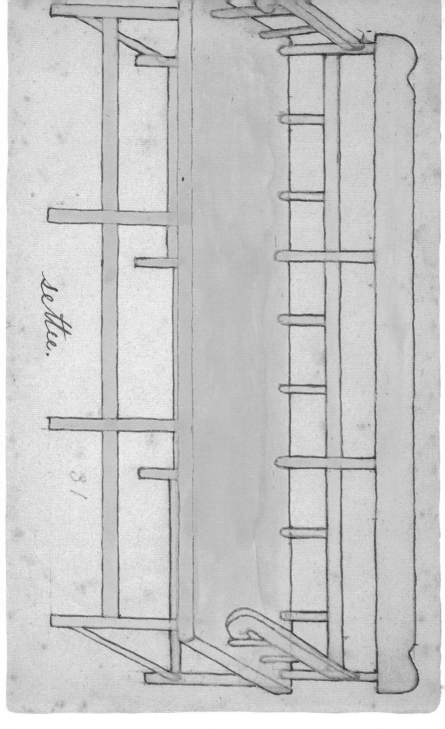

settee.

31

PLATE 17

BENCH

The smaller bench is an enlargement of one seen in stool size, Plate 8. It is shown doubled again at the top. Gray was a church bench color; green, for a front porch.

ROCKING CHAIR

These armchair and side-chair rockers, showing spindle-back and ladder-back types, were typical of the country chairmaker's craft. They have flat plank seats and rockers resembling those on Lapp's cradles.

Bench

Rocking chair

PLATE 18

LADDER

These are two traditional forms of the useful ladder. The eight-foot triangular stepladder is sturdy and free-standing, while the simpler twelve-foot ladder needs a firm footing and a gentle "lean" to assure a safe climb.

39

8 Feet

12 Feet

extention step Ladder

PLATE 19

LADDER

Extension ladders, with block and pulley raising and lowering mechanisms, could be handled by one man and were extensively used in housebuilding, roofing, or inside barns to gain access to lofts. The fifteen-foot ladder at the right was designed especially for picking fruit. It is wide at the bottom for stability and narrow at the top to fit into the branches of fruit trees. Such ladders are still in use.

41

41

42

28 Feet

15 Feet

Ladder

PLATE 20

WOOD CHESTS

Dovetailed for strength at the corners, these wood chests, or chists as they were pronounced in Pennsylvania German dialect, had interior dividers to separate kindling from fuel logs. The lids, double hinged and overhung for finger grip, raised or lowered separately. The two chests are alike except for the addition of fancy turned feet in the second example.

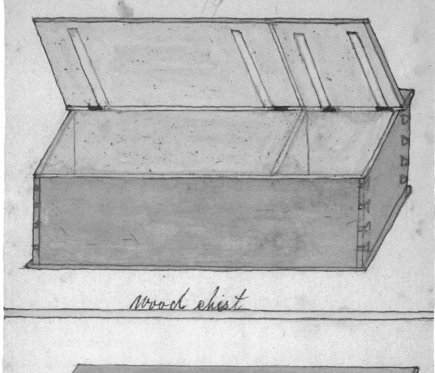

Wood chist

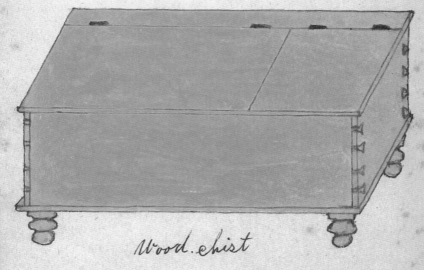

Wood. chist

PLATE 21

APPARATUS FOR WASHING DAY

Amish farmlands were stripped of trees to provide as much planting ground as possible. Thus, the clothes drying rack was essential household equipment and was probably made at home unless Henry Lapp's special design caught the fancy.

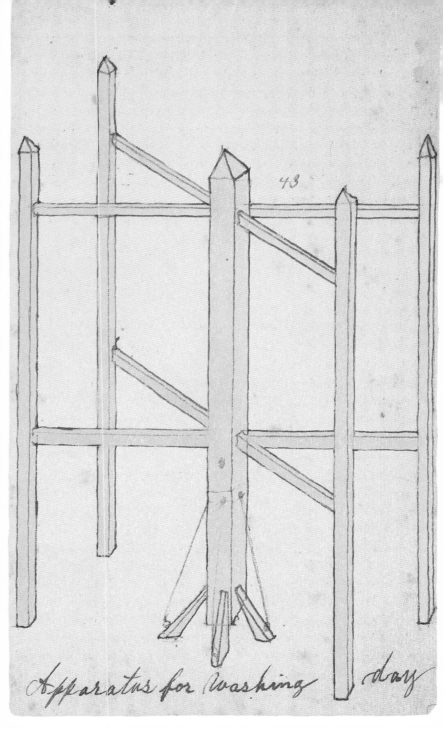

43

Apparatus for washing day

APPARATUS FOR WASHING DAY

This shape is used as much today as in the mid-nineteenth century. Its versatile collapsible frame and light portable weight are evident.

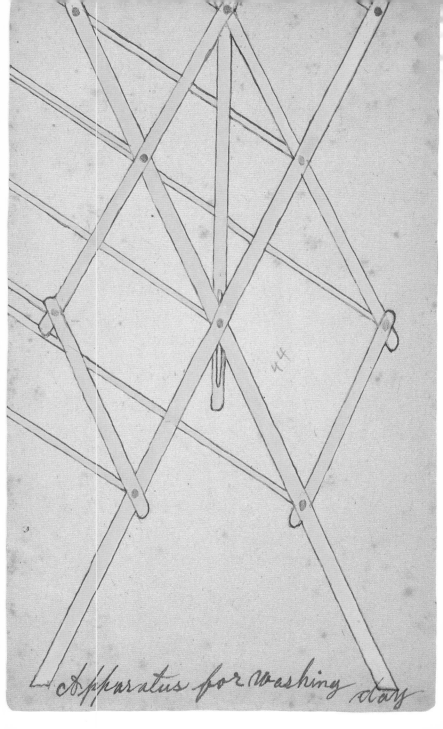

Apparatus for washing day

PLATE 23

DESK

The interior view of this desk with the writing flap down shows the storage well. The open cubbyhole section above would indicate that the desk was used in a store or post office. The long key protruding from its escutcheon firmly secured the interior contents.

BROOM HANDLE

Small, round dowels bound tightly together made large broom handles to which sweeping heads made of broom corn were attached.

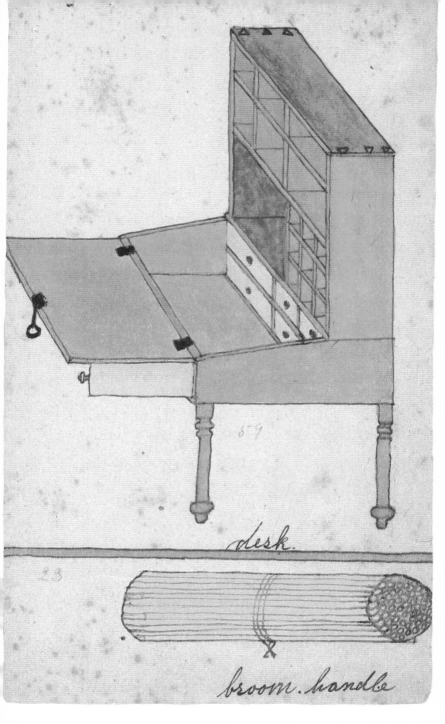

desk.

broom. handle

PLATE 24

STEP LADDER

This type of ladder was used by painters and plasterers who could insert planks between two of them and "walk a wall."

❋

BEE BOX

Along with fruits and vegetables, honey was coveted and garnered by the farmer. These boxes served as man-made supports in which the beehive could fasten its honeycomb. They allowed some portability and access to the interior by the cautious farmer. Nailed together, sometimes dovetailed, the bee box was a home product built with care for its purpose rather than beauty.

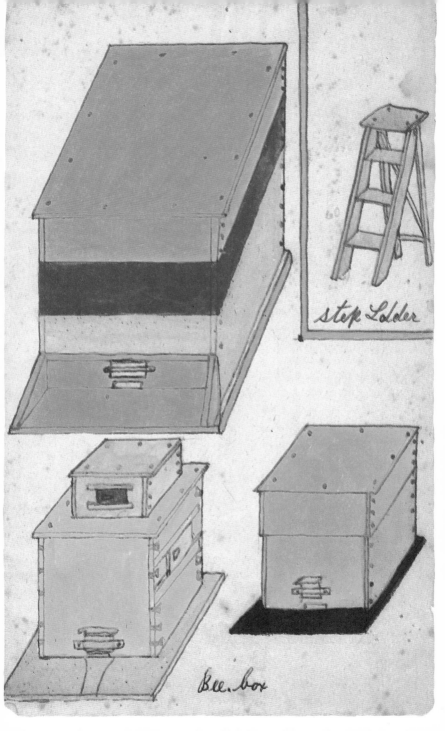

step Ladder

Bee box

PLATE 25

DRAWER

The centered looking glass suggests that this chunky design for a bureau, or chest of drawers, was intended for bedroom or dressing use. Henry Lapp's formula for construction and color accentuates the solidity of this piece.

❊

DRAWER

Simpler than the above, this is probably a washstand. Cupboards instead of drawers, and pegs set into the splashboard on which to hang brushes or towels, indicate its use. The same general proportions and color as the above piece suggest Lapp may have intended a bedroom suite, but none of Lapp's designs show a matching bed. Suites, or room sets, were very popular in the nineteenth century and were sold throughout the country by mail order as well as in high-style centers.

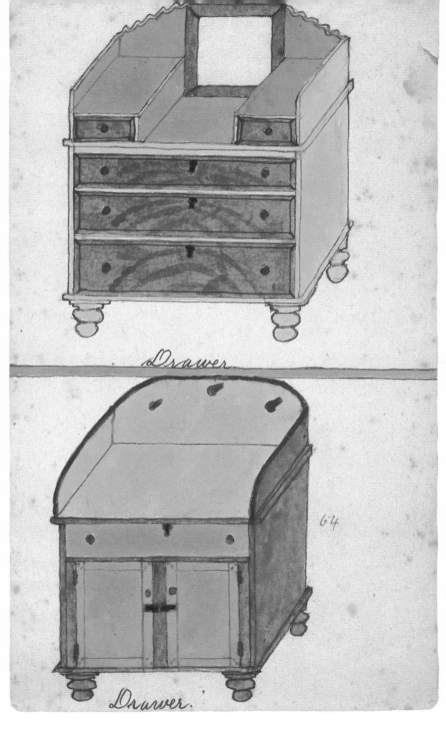

Drawer.

64

Drawer.

PLATE 26

LITTLE TABLE

Two variations on a theme—customer's choice. Legs have become ring-turned where incised lines had formerly been the case, and the feet are simple round balls instead of carrot feet. The table on the left is straightforward with one drawer; that on the right allows concealed locked storage space, the back top being hinged to the table frame.

❋

CHEST

Probably small, this flat-topped chest was built for home or store use.

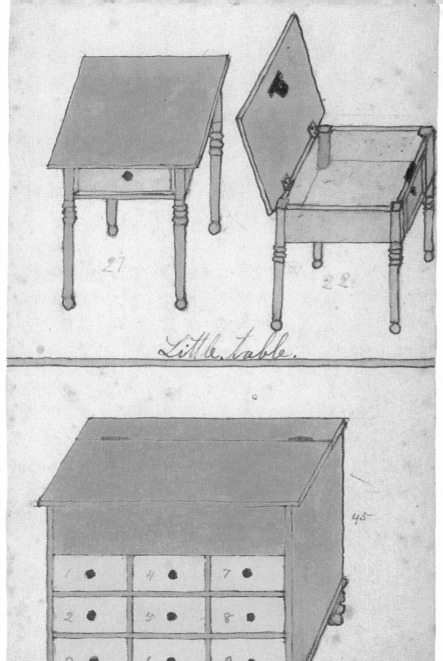

27

22

Little table.

45

1	4	7
2	5	8
3	6	9

Chist

PLATE 27

CHEST; BIN

Although unlabeled, the chest, probably very small, with six drawers, and the little bin with a sloping lid, were designed for general home and store use.

ROSE BOX; LEMON BOX

These portable and movable boxes were used for gathering and storing fruits and vegetables. Only recently have collectors discovered their suitability as planters.

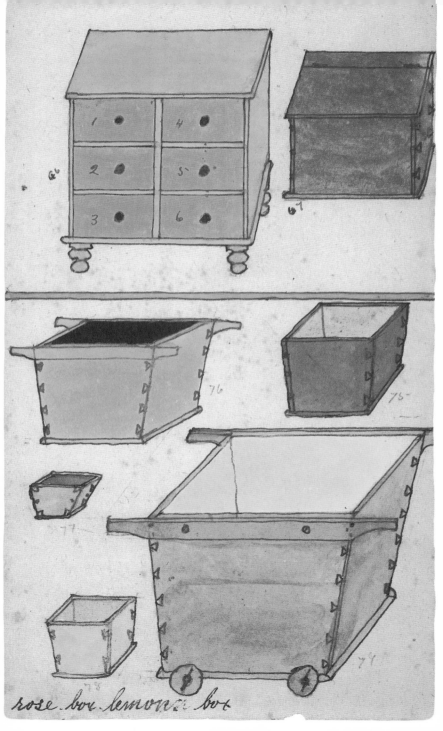

66

67

76

75

77

73

74

78

rose box   lemon box

PLATE 28

SEED DRAWER

Well carpentered, colorfully painted, and strictly utilitarian, these seed storage boxes hung on the walls of kitchens and barns, general and hardware stores. Numbered drawers, sometimes of varying sizes, helped to organize the tiny seeds for planting or when gathered.

NAILS

Similar units of drawers were made by Lapp to hold nails. As every repair or building project involving the use of wood required nails, a wide variety of size and type were routine hardware store supplies. These drawers were used at home as well as in stores.

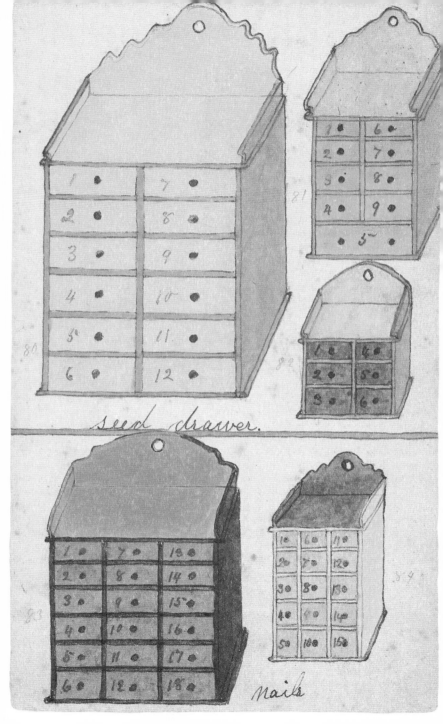

seed drawer.

nails

PLATE 29

FLOWER STAND

A standard form using neat but plain construction, these stands are made today for the same purpose—to display and sell summer produce by the roadside.

❁

TRELLIS

Resembling his design for washday apparatus, Lapp's trellis could support a mighty rose.

❁

FLOWER STAND

A rounded flower stand shows Lapp's version of adjustable shelves which rest on the serrated edge of the front support. These stands were usually painted; green was their customary color.

Flower stand

Trellis

Flowerstand.

PLATE 30

TRELLIS

Of the seven designs for ornamental trellises, Lapp's circular form on the lower right is most unusual.

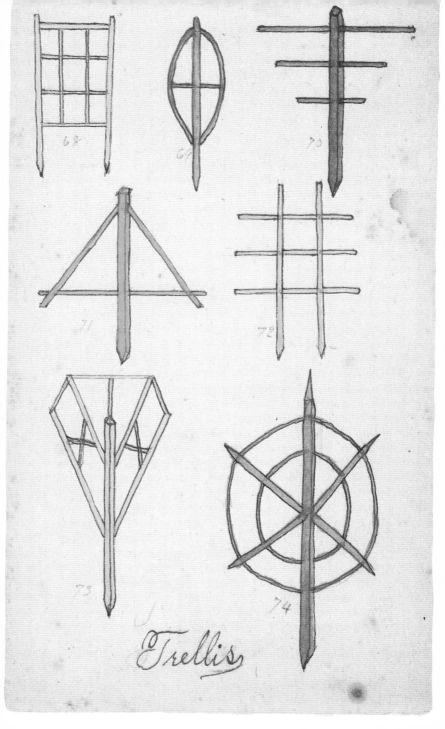

Trellis

PLATE 31

PUZZLE BLOCKS

Puzzle becomes pizzle according to Lapp's phonetic spelling. Ageless and seemingly endless, puzzle blocks were teasers for young and old alike. The aim was to get all the numbers in order without lifting any block from the box and to leave the empty space only at the beginning or end.

HANDLES

A Lapp descendant in the woodworking trade says of these pieces: "What you see are different sizes of round handles or dowels which are worked out for different uses such as play pens and baby cribs. The small bundle could be match sticks which I still remember were used to move fire from stove to oil lamps instead of striking a new match which in early days were expensive and possibly not too many around."

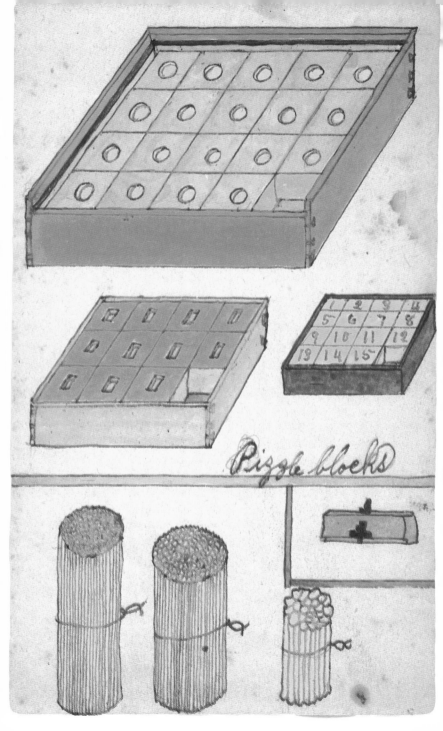

Puzzle blocks

PLATE 32

GREAT COUNTER

This piece was probably designed to be the main counter in a hardware store, possibly Lapp's own. Handy numbered drawers held all kinds and sizes of fittings, and the long top surface provided unencumbered work space. It is painted in the typical red and blue-gray found on dower chests of the Pennsylvania Germans.

great counter.

PLATE 33

DRAWER

This unit with drawers and cubbyholes, top, was an "organizer" for home or store.

❁

SPOON BOX

Cutlery was stored or carried about in a variety of containers, the most familiar being the double-sided open box with handle. Others hung on the wall, like the seed and nail units. As spoons were well cared for, their containers were neatly finished with dovetailing and, sometimes, curved backpieces for hanging.

❁

FLOUR SHOVEL

Two forms of this much-used utensil suggest they are of wood rather than tin. They were stored in the bottom of the flour chest along with the dough tray.

❁

COUNTERS

Simple counting devices, lower right, probably kept track of an inventory, whether quarts or barrels, gallons or hogsheads, at home or in a store.

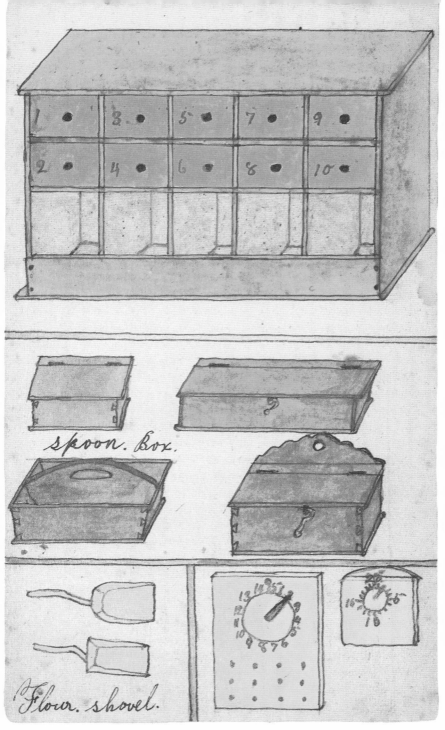

spoon. Box.

Flour. shovel.

PLATE 34

GAMES

Amusements made with string and wire are centuries old and perhaps began as knots and novelties made by sailors on long voyages. The flip-flop, upper left, is an ageless wonder for the young; and the various wire configurations illustrated challenge the player to extricate the "trapped" piece, usually a circle, without bending or changing the shape of the original figure. The piece at the lower right appears in Pennsylvania German forms and traces back to old Germany and Scandinavia—swing the weight and the chickens peck!

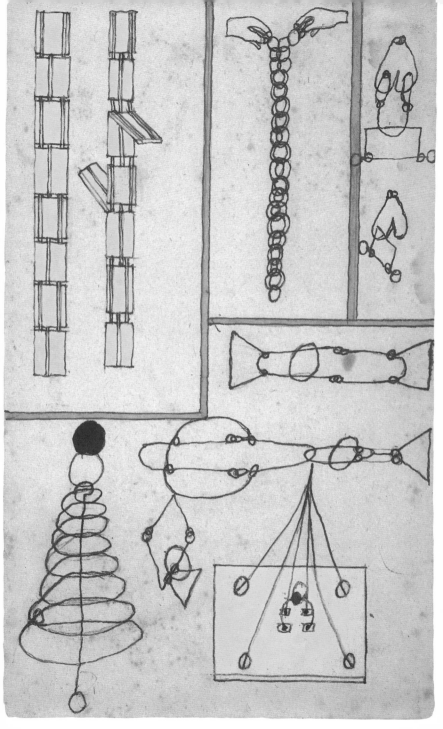

PLATE 35

PICTURE FRAMES

Although Pennsylvania Germans did not frame and display their family records, preferring to fold them into Bibles or glue them into dower chests, they did frame samplers, prints, hand-colored printed records, and paintings. Lapp's frames and the fanciful suggestions he makes for pictures to frame would have been popular at the end of the nineteenth century when prints, calendars, even silhouettes, were available to rural and urban customers alike. The same frames were suitable for looking glasses, and each home probably had at least one, however small.

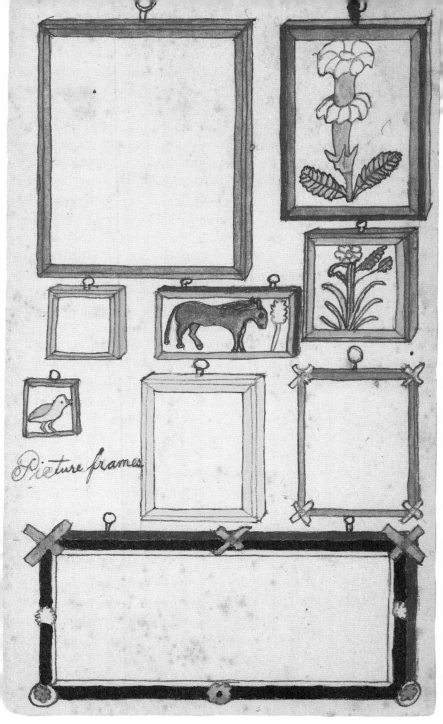

Picture frames

PLATE 36

SLEIGH

Lapp was known to have made the wood part of the sleigh and the boxes for Amish buggies. His drawings probably reveal little about his crafting of these large, somewhat complicated pieces, except for the dovetailing which appears enormous on the sleigh.

❋

BUGGY BOX

The manufacture of the buggy required the efforts of several craftsmen. Henry Lapp cabinetmaker made the jaunty box; the blacksmith forged springs and fittings; and the wheelwright installed the large spoked wheels. They were light and smooth-running vehicles, drawn by one horse.

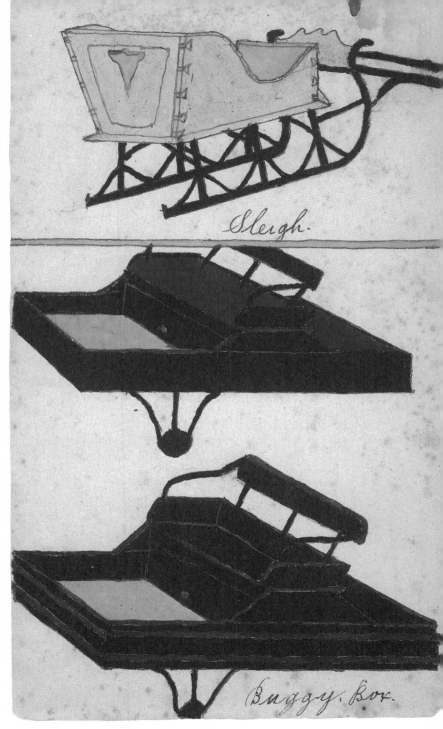

Sleigh.

Buggy. Box.

PLATE 37

MOUSE TRAPS

Although the cage illustrated at the upper left might have help a pet mouse, it was more likely for a red squirrel, long a favorite children's pet. The other four devices suggest their ingenuity with reasonable clarity, being variously rigged to spring upon the unsuspecting rodent. The large one at the upper right, called a "dead fall" trap, was made for rats or mice depending upon the size and weight of the falling plank. Made with care and precision in order to achieve their purpose, these traditional forms were rarely improved upon—they worked or they didn't!

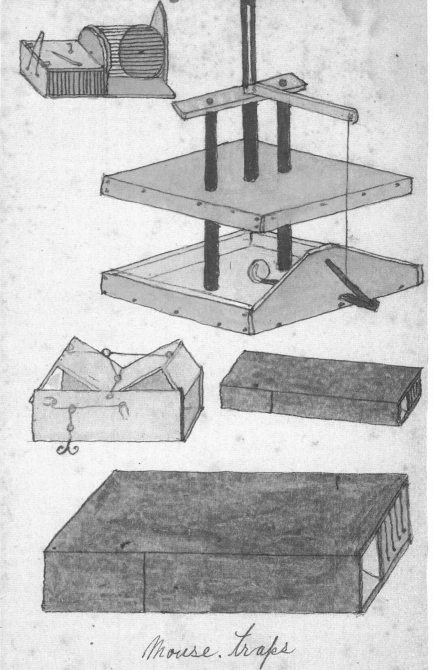

Mouse. Traps

PLATE 38

EGG BEATER

This wire device spun first one way and then the other by pumping the handle.

❁

SALAD SOWER

With spikes to mark rows, this hand-drawn sower was used to scatter the very fine seeds of lettuce or tobacco.

❁

BREAD TOASTER

Bread was fitted between the wire coils and held near the fire or stove until browned. The ring on the handle tightened the hold on the bread.

❁

At the top of the page is a divided cutlery box; in the middle, two pie crimpers.

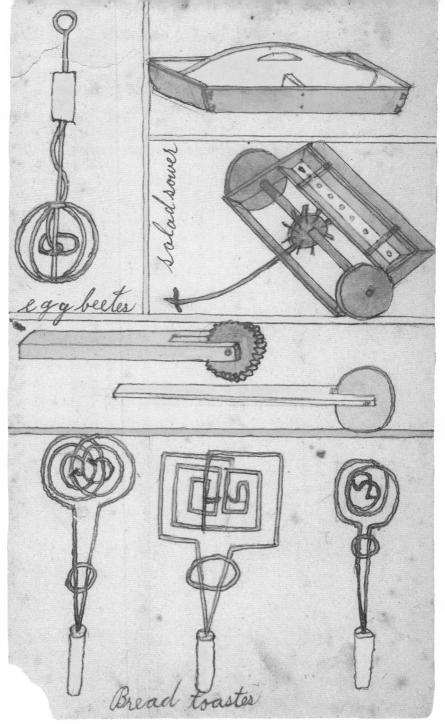

egg beeter

salad sower

Bread toaster

PLATE 39

COMB BOX
Conveniently hung by the washstand or near a looking glass, the slanted shelves of the comb box held the household supply.

✸

LITTLE FANNING MILLS
Turned at high speed with the side handle, this mechanical device separated wheat from chaff. It was easily accomplished by a child at home.

✸

ROLLING PINS
Two of an endless variety of handle designs for the baker's necessity, the rolling pin was used to flatten dough for cookies and pies. None of Lapp's designs concern themselves with the "decorative" baking of shaped cookies, or springerle, which required special pastry doughs or molds.

✸

BOXES
Trinkets, ribbons, or other small treasures could be gathered together and securely locked in these different-sized boxes. The largest box, right, might have held important papers.

✸

SPITTING BOX
The spittoon was usually filled with sand or sawdust to absorb the residue from tobacco chewers.

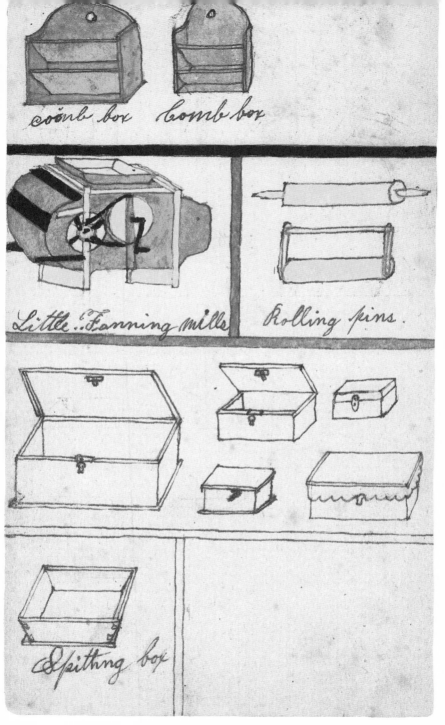

comb box   Comb box

Little Fanning Mills   Rolling pins

Spithing box

PLATE 40

LITTLE THRASHMACHINE

Although unmistakably a Lapp creation, the portable threshing machine was known in Lancaster County by 1832, some of Lancaster manufacture, some imported from Northumberland County. They had spiked cylinders connected by leather straps and pulleys which were geared into a cast-iron shaft to which horses were hitched for power.

Little. Thrashmachine

PLATE 41

JUMPING JACKS

The funny men leap over and over when you squeeze their supports, or they tumble or seesaw or flip! They have been entertaining children for centuries and appeared in Europe and England made by woodworkers and sold by itinerant peddlers.

CALCULATORS

One could wish Henry Lapp had titled this illustration. It is probably a counter used in a mill to tally grain received, grain milled, and grain withheld as the miller's payment. The dial, which could be moved by releasing the ratchet mechanism, lower left, was set at the number of bushels (up to twenty) which the farmer brought to be ground; and the pegs inserted into the holes kept track of the bags of flour. Thus the dial could be reset after the first twenty bushels were milled, and the farmer's account kept on the board at least until he had sixteen bags of flour. It was called "tolling the farmer's wheat." The calculator on the right, a simpler version, lacks the ratchet mechanism for the dial.

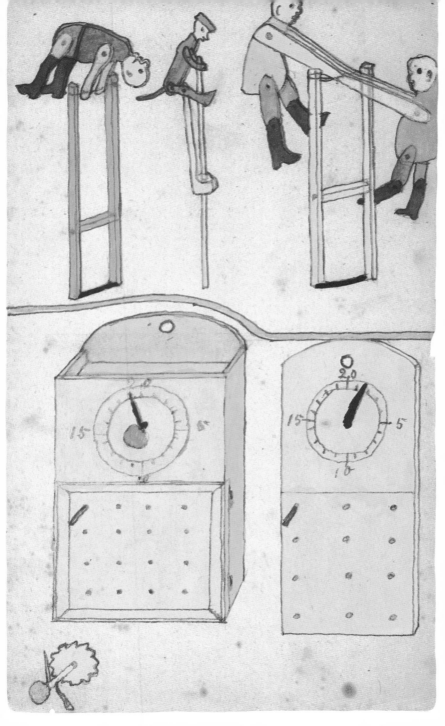

PLATE 42

LITTLE WAGON

Skilled carpenters were often called upon to build or repair the farmer's heavy hauling wagons. So too they made child-sized wagons, using the same construction details, for use and amusement.

WHEELBARROW

The shape of the wheelbarrow remains the same today with minor variations depending upon the task to be performed. But alas Henry Lapp's color schemes have faded.

Little wagon.

Wheelbarrow

PLATE 43

LITTLE HOUSE

The windows and corner turrets on this brightly colored doll house are puzzling. It might be a barn or a castle—or perhaps Henry Lapp had visited the 1876 Centennial Exposition and was inspired by one of the exotic pavilions.

❂

LOOKING GLASS

Dressing stands with swinging mirrors were placed on bureaus and washstands, with the comb box close by.

Little house.

looking glass.

PLATE 44

MOUSE TRAPS

The clever designs of these devices coped with more than one mouse per night.

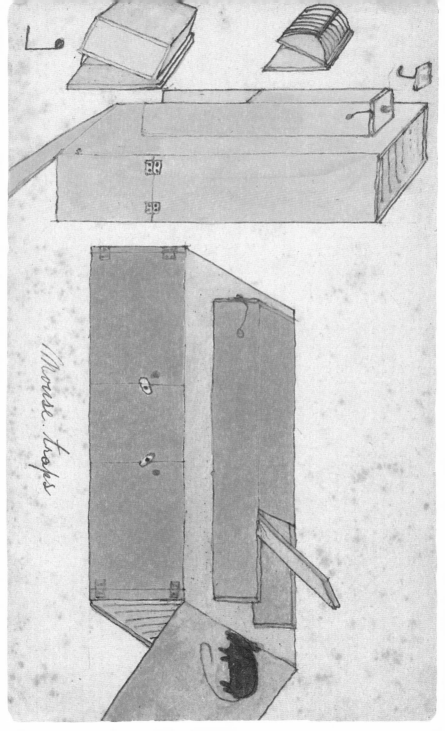

Mouse traps

PLATE 45

DOMINOES

Fitted neatly into a box, wooden domino blocks and the games derived from them made fine use of the leftover bits of wood which gather in all carpentry shops. So too the gaily painted complete village, with church, town hall, houses, and fencing, nestled in its own box, was both a toy and a puzzle. A push-pull rattle, small wagon, step stool, mini-table and chair, were treasured children's possessions.

dominoes

PLATE 46

LITTLE CHEST

Three versions of the form of small chest offered the customer varying degrees of finish as well as versatility.

❁

MILK CUPBOARD

Large pans for skimming cream, ladles, small churns, even cheese presses, would have been scrubbed clean and stored together in a unit such as this milk cupboard.

❁

WALL SHELVES

Hanging shelves were used for everything from wooden matches to the best ornamental ceramics. Easily made, they were decorative accessories in most shops.

❁

SCOUR BOX

Knives and cutlery were rubbed hard against soft stone in the scour box, after which the utensils were rinsed, dried, and stored in cutlery boxes.

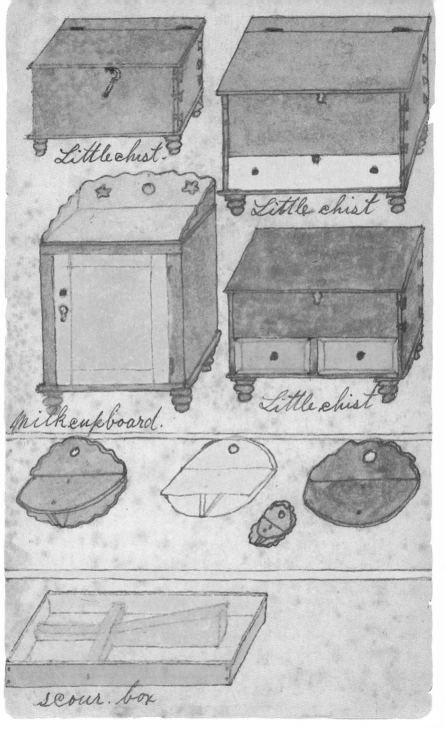

Little chist.

Little chist

Milk cupboard.

Little chist

scour. box

PLATE 47

RABBIT TRAPS

Rabbits ate young plants in the garden, hence their meat was delicious in stews and pies. Traps were used in preference to guns, and their mechanisms worked like the smaller devices designed for mice.

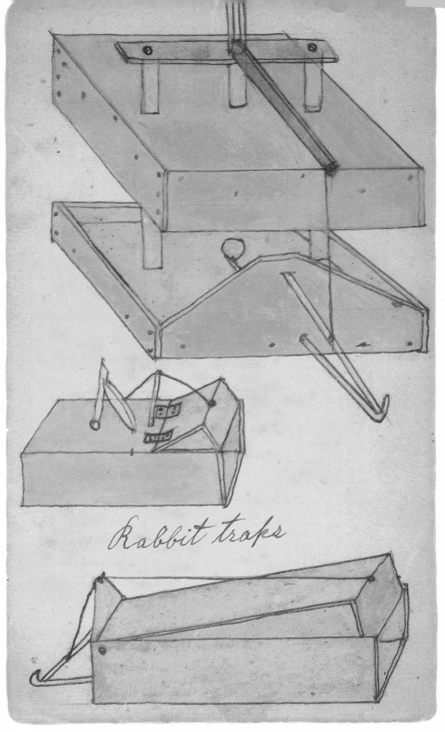

Rabbit traps